MW01100385

Letters and Sounds

Ww, Xx

SCHOOL PUBLISHERS

Photos:
p. 2, © Harcourt Telescope; p. 3, © Harcourt Index; p. 4, © Harcourt Telescope; p. 5, © Superstock; p. 6, © Harcourt Telescope; p. 7, © Shutterstock; p. 8, © Harcourt Telescope.

Printed in China

ISBN-13: 978-0-15-358376-6
ISBN-10: 0-15-358376-2

Ordering Options
ISBN 10: 0-15-358355-X (Grade K Below-Level Collection)
ISBN 13: 978-0-15-358355-1 (Grade K Below-Level Collection)
ISBN 10: 0-15-360629-0 (package of 5)
ISBN 13: 978-0-15-360629-8 (package of 5)

4 5 6 7 8 9 10 0940 15 14 13 12 11 10 09

W

W

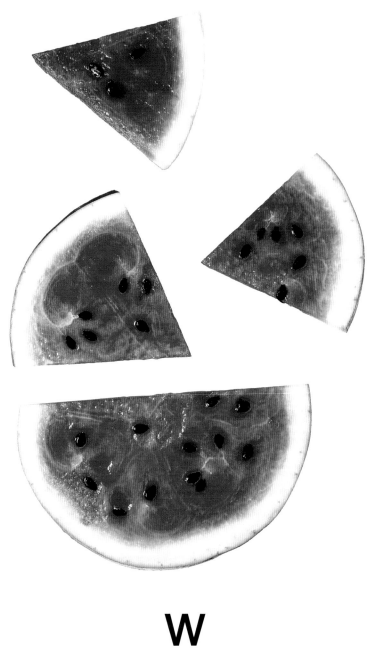

W

W

fox

OX

box